The Teleprompter Manual

For executives, politicians,
broadcasters & speakers

*To the best of the best
all my love
Jamie*

Everything you need to know to be natural, confident & powerful when addressing any size audience, anytime, anywhere.

The Teleprompter Manual

For executives, politicians, broadcasters & speakers

By Laurie Brown

Published by
The Difference Press
P.O. Box 69046
Pleasant Ridge, Michigan 48069

This book is available at special quantity discounts to use as premiums
and sales promotions, or to use in corporate training programs. For more
information contact the author at Lauriebrown@thedifference.net, call
877.999.3433 or contact your local bookstore.

Printed in the United States of America.
1st printing 2006

Library of Congress Control Number: 2005905300
ISBN 10: 0-9767761-0-3
ISBN 13: 978-0-9767761-0-9

Jacket and book design by Eric Keller
Illustrations by Daniel Keller

To Hubert "Hub" Schlafly

Contents

The Teleprompter Manual

Acknowledgements

CREATING THIS BOOK SHOWED ME that the single name of an author on a cover is an oversimplification. This book took the expertise and generosity of many people to whom I'm deeply indebted.

First and foremost, I want to thank Cindy Schmidt who taught me what a great teleprompter operator does. Thanks to Linda Hurd, for her knowledge, experience and writing skills, as well as a deep and lasting friendship, which were the backbone of this work; my brother, Manny, who continually inspires me; Peggy Thorp who provided love and support as well as a keen eye for grammatical errors; Mary Locker, for believing in me when I couldn't.

Thank you to: Bill Moore, Emily Schreiber-Moore, Eileen Polk, Curt Dombecky, Jon Quade, Karen Keller, Greg Jones, Leslie Charles, Sam Horn, and Loretta Higgins for their suggestions and friendship; all the girls in the photo; the folks at CBTV, Tim Murphy, Eric Walker and Laurie Stout for their technical advice.

Further thanks to Fanny Wheeler who helped me find Mr. Schlafly; Paul Manzella; my dearest friends Bruce Economou and Monica Deeter; and of course, everyone listed in the resource section and countless others.

A special thank you to Eric Keller, for graphic design as well as his patience and support, and to Daniel Keller for the drawings.

Perhaps the best part of writing this book was reconnecting with a great friend and brilliant editor, Sheri Stein. The days that we spent poring over the words were some of the best in recent memory.

Foreword

NEVER UNDERESTIMATE the symbiotic relationship between man and machine. Reading from a teleprompter sounds easy — Wrong! It's a skill that takes great technique, and without that, the machine wins every time — usually operated by a person named Stuart who is scrolling the data too fast.

If you learn to make the teleprompter your friend, you will be able to create the illusion that you are a brilliant and extemporaneous orator and audience members will most likely want to nominate you for a Nobel Prize — ok, ok, they will at least enjoy what you have to say because you'll actually feel comfortable. It's truly a 'power' tool.

This book is full of tips that took me a long time to learn on my own through trial and error. I've known Laurie Brown for years as we cut our teeth together in commercials and the exciting world of industrials where the teleprompter is your only real friend. Laurie really knows the ins and outs. I might add, she also throws crazy costume parties where we all…. (I would continue, but the teleprompter operator just left for lunch.)

> — Tim Allen, Actor/Writer/Producer,
> *Home Improvement (TV), Galaxy Quest, Toy Story,*
> *The Shaggy Dog, The Santa Clause…*

Introduction

I CONSIDER MYSELF REMARKABLY LUCKY to earn a living as a sales and presentation skills trainer and consultant, doing what I love. However, I didn't arrive at this point through a direct career path. I began as an actor primarily performing onstage but also doing commercials and films. Since I lived in Detroit, much of the available film work involved auto industry training films geared to workers, executives, and auto dealerships. It was during this period that I discovered the teleprompter, and believe me, it proved to be a life-saver. Without it, I would have spent countless hours memorizing long and often difficult scripts. Besides sparing me that time, the teleprompter made the film sessions far more productive — speakers working from memory invariably forget lines and have to do retakes — which saved money for the companies that hired me.

I distinctly remember the first time I had the chance to use the teleprompter. My agent called to let me know that I had gotten a job and that I wouldn't need to memorize 20 pages of technical jargon. I was ecstatic… no memorization. I expected using the teleprompter to be a breeze. After all, how hard could it be to read? I certainly wasn't prepared for the skill it took to read the script, sound natural, and not look like a deer caught in the headlights. I had to learn through trial and error. It took time and experience to grasp the technical elements and nuances in performance that now make my presentations more effective.

Learning to use the teleprompter is not difficult, but to gain control of the system, to transform the teleprompter from a slightly awkward convenience to a tool of power, requires understanding enough small points to fill a book — in fact, the very one you're holding. If I had understood the basics explained in this manual, I would have saved a lot of time — and one or two embarrassing presentations. This book is the one I wish had been available to me.

I LIKE TO TELL PEOPLE about the history of the teleprompter. First of all, it's an amazing device that, like many inventions, sprang from a quirky beginning. Secondly, I recently had the great pleasure of hearing the story firsthand from Hubert "Hub" Schlafly, one of the teleprompter's co-inventors, when I interviewed him at his home in Connecticut. Mr. Schlafly is a remarkable man. He was a pioneer of television technology, receiving two Emmy awards for his contributions. His work has also involved major developments in cable broadcasting and significant advances in military technology. The holder of 16 patents, Mr. Schlafly is still inventing at the age of 85.

The story as Hub tells it: In 1950, an actor named Fred Barton was appearing nightly on Broadway in a production of *Mr. Roberts* with Henry Fonda when he also was hired to perform on television. Although Barton was accustomed to memorizing his lines for plays, television demanded he learn a new set of skills. For stage work, Barton memorized one script and repeated his lines every night. With television, which at the time was performed live, each episode required an entirely different script — and Barton found that with his full schedule, he had almost no time to learn his parts. During this era, prompting devices for actors did exist, including cue cards and radio receivers hidden in the ear, but Barton was dissatisfied with all of them.

Once Barton grew more familiar with the nature of live television, he was able to envision a device with, as he has explained, "multiple outlets with synchronized display of the actors' lines." He soon brought his idea to Irving Berlin Kahn (the nephew of the composer) at Twentieth Century Fox. Kahn contacted Hub Schlafly, the studio's director of TV research. Once the three men considered the idea, they realized it was not just possible, but possibly lucrative. They decided to go into business together, forming the TelePrompTer Corporation and creating the first teleprompter.

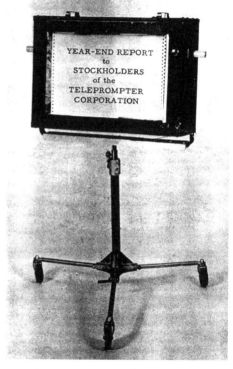

Essentially, their invention was a "suitcase" with holes cut into the sides. The lines appeared on a motorized "Roman Scroll" visible through one of the holes. Schlafly describes the initial version as a "40 lb. monster."

Every script had to be hand typed on a special typewriter that the Underwood Company produced. The type was three-eighths or one-half inch high. Often typists were hired to work through the night to meet the demands of live television. According to Schlafly, the typing was dangerous work. For some reason, the keys would fly off the typewriter and zip across the room like shrapnel. Apparently, nobody was lost in the process. However, one night while the crew was typing away, there was so much noise that the whole staff was arrested for disturbing the peace and had to be bailed out of jail the next morning.

In a 1952 article written by Fred Barton and H. J. Schlafly for the Society of Motion Picture and Television Engineers, they stated: "The problem of presenting entertainment to the public has been accentuated by the very nature of the television industry because of its continual requirement for new material. Added to the tension that normally accompanies the production of a television or motion picture presentation is the very real and continuing chore of memorization of lines for the actor, and the constant threat of fluffs, delays and retakes for the producer. A professional performer accepts, as part of his vocation, the necessity of studying his lines. Such a professional can substantially memorize new material with comparatively few readings, but in order to reach the point of perfection, the point which makes the difference between a smooth and a ragged performance, this same actor may spend many tedious hours of study. Those who are not normally engaged in the entertainment or public speaking professions find this problem of memory so much the more difficult. The necessity for accurate memorization breeds a second evil, which may be even more devastating to a good performance than the mere fault of forgetting the line. This second evil is the fear of forgetting the lines and the resulting tension, tightness and unnaturalness unconsciously generated by such a fear."

The industry embraced the new technology and used it on such productions as the Milton Berle Texaco Star Theatre and a soap opera called *The First Hundred Years*. Apparently, one feature of the teleprompter made Berle's show an often frantic scene. Once the teleprompter was in place on the set, any script corrections had to be made manually, by taping over the old copy and writing in the changes by hand. This kept the company's team of stagehands running, because Berle used six prompters on his set and typically made changes up until the last minute.

In 1952, Business Week published an article on the teleprompter. Soon after, Hub Schlafly remembers getting a call from someone identified only as the "Chief". Evidently this person had read the article and wanted Schlafly to come to the Waldorf Astoria, where he was staying, and give a demonstration. When Schlafly arrived at the hotel, he discovered that the Chief was none other than President Herbert Hoover. After seeing how the device operated, Hoover immediately realized what the teleprompter could do for his presentations and decided he would use it to deliver his keynote address at the upcoming Republican Convention in Chicago.

Interestingly, Hoover's decision wound up giving the teleprompter the best publicity its inventors could have ever wanted. Schlafly had carefully explained to Hoover that the teleprompter would move at his pace, allowing him to stop, ad-lib, and then return to his speech.

Nevertheless, when Hoover threw in an ad-lib and the scroll stopped moving, he panicked and called out to ask what was wrong with the teleprompter. With the President shouting the name TelePrompTer in front of such an important audience, the invention received a boost of national publicity. In fact, Hoover's Republican audience so instantly grasped the value of the teleprompter that politicians requested it for 48 of the convention speeches.

.

At that point, the teleprompter took off. 1952 became a banner year for the company, which formed TelePrompTer International as a subsidiary of the TelePrompTer Corporation. The business began leasing equipment in Mexico and negotiating deals in Europe, South America, and Cuba. Meanwhile, teleprompter use in this country continued to boom as people in a widening variety of fields recognized the device's merits. Some famous customers of the period included: Arthur Godfrey; Gov. Paul Dever (for his hour and 10 minute "ad-lib" speech as a Democratic keynote speaker); President Eisenhower (who used it throughout his campaign); General Motors (for coverage of its executive conference); Cardinal Spellman; the cast of Dragnet; Betty Furness; and Ed Sullivan.

The company's next step involved further refinements of the technology. Schlafly describes how it came about: "Encouraged by the popularity of the device for public speaking, we became aware that a less obtrusive means of presenting the text for use at a speaker's podium would be highly desirable. We developed a 'one way mirror' device we called the Speech View system. Bausch & Lomb laboratories provided us with a molecular coating for glass to improve the reflective quality. The prompter, hidden in the base, reflected the

For Your Convention Speech

YOUR COMMITTEE HAS RETAINED

TELEPROMPTER CORPORATION

PROVIDING YOU WITH

A specially designed speaker's platform and specially designed speaking facilities

THE DEMOCRATIC NATIONAL CONVENTION

AUG. 13 to 17, 1956   International Amphitheatre, Chicago

text on the glass to the speaker while the audience looked through the glass without being aware of the text. Two such prompters, one on the right and one on the left of the speaker allowed him to switch from one to the other and appear to address the entire audience."

The company went on to develop a speaker's podium that included two synchronized teleprompter reading units, desk lighting, a clock, air conditioning outlets, and an adjustable-height speaker's platform. The Democrats used this new device during their 1956 National Convention. The success of the company's public-speaking system led to a revised model for on-camera use. Schlafly explains that the new technology was based on the "same optical principle, [which was] mounted on the camera directly in front of the lens. The camera looked through the glass; the performer looked directly at the TV audience and was able to read the text word for word. This device now has world wide use."

6

PHOTOGRAPH COURTESY OF HUBERT SCHLAFLY

Singer Patrice Munsel *checks her TelePrompTer script before the Ingemar Johanson-Floyd Patterson fight in 1959.*

In the early 1960s, the TelePrompTer Corporation sold the prompting side of the business but held on to the name as it expanded into broader areas of communication. The company became involved in television programming for heavyweight boxing championships and auto racing, designed control rooms for the military, and eventually shifted into cable television systems. In fact, in 1973, Schlafly and Kahn demonstrated the very first domestic satellite transmission of a cable program to a convention of cable operators, from Washington, D.C. to Anaheim, California.

7

Through the years, the teleprompter has become an essential component for many divergent fields, while remaining integral to television entertainment. In 1980, the National Academy of Television Arts and Sciences, recognizing the tremendous contribution of the on-camera teleprompter, awarded its inventors an Emmy. Today, not only TV stations, but also various departments of the government and many corporations maintain in-house prompting staffs. The device has become indispensable for a growing number of politicians and executives. Even famous bands are learning to rely on teleprompters during live performances.

Of course, the teleprompter system has changed along with the prevailing technology. An electronic system with a computer has replaced the "Roman Scroll" teleprompter, and shooting typewriter keys no longer threaten roomfuls of typists. New companies continue to emerge worldwide developing remarkable advancements. Despite any changes, though, Barton, Kahn, and Schlafly's original intent is still evident: to simplify presenters' lives and empower them to communicate directly to their audience.

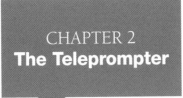

CHAPTER 2
The Teleprompter

IT'S HELPFUL TO UNDERSTAND that the word "teleprompter" is used rather loosely. Though it often seems to refer to a single unit, in actuality, you'll be dealing with a system whose components vary slightly according to the circumstances of your presentation.

For the most part, you will be dealing directly with two components of a teleprompter system: a monitor and a separate screen. The computer monitor will display the text of your presentation, which will scroll vertically at your particular speaking pace. Most of the time, you will not be looking directly at the monitor but at a one-way mirror that clearly reflects the monitor's display of your script.

There is one element of the teleprompter system that remains constant: the human element. No matter the type of teleprompter, you will always be working with a teleprompter operator. This person is the professional who runs the show and whose expertise will, to a large extent, determine the quality of your presentation. We'll discuss your interaction with the teleprompter operator in great detail further along.

9

There are basically three types of teleprompters. Which one you use will depend upon your location and the kind of presentation you're giving. These are the main considerations:

- Will your presentation be on camera or in front of a live audience?
- Will you be indoors or out?
- If indoors, what is the size of the room where you'll be speaking?
- If outdoors, how large an area will you need to cover?

Types of Teleprompters

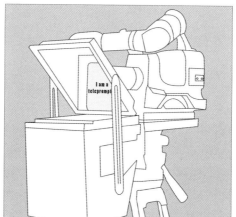

On-camera prompter

On-camera Prompter

When you appear on camera, you will use a teleprompter system with a monitor mounted just below the camera lens. However, you will not actually be looking at the monitor but at a piece of specialized glass. The glass is positioned in front of the camera lens and placed on an angle so that it reflects your scrolling script. This glass is what allows you to look directly into the lens while you read. The glass is invisible to the camera and to the viewer. A pointer will indicate the line that you should be reading. Often a hood is placed over the prompter mirror to protect the glass from reflecting the studio lights.

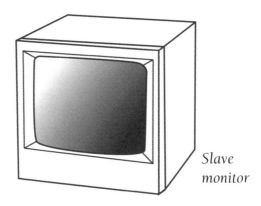

Slave monitor

Slave Monitors

There are times while working on camera when you will need to turn away from your camera to demonstrate something or to speak with other people involved in the presentation. The monitor is actually a television display — sometimes a flat LCD or plasma screen. When you turn away, you'll then read your script directly from one or more of the other monitors (known as "slave monitors"), which are placed in your line of vision. The additional monitors allow you to maintain the illusion that you are speaking spontaneously.

Presidential Prompters

When you speak to a live audience, you will most likely use what's called a "presidential prompter". In this case, you'll read from a glass plate that reflects your scrolling script from a monitor that is placed

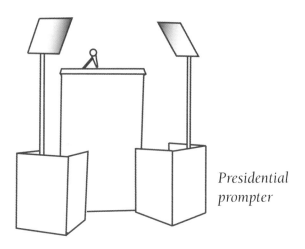

Presidential prompter

on the floor and directed upward. The plate is mounted on a pole and angled to reflect the image from the monitor on the floor. The monitor and glass plate can be placed close to the speaker, since the audience can look through the glass plate without seeing the script. The height of the plate can be adjusted to your eye level, which allows for good eye contact. This is a more formal type of system that will lock you behind the podium.

Indoor Presentation

When making an indoor live presentation, you can use either large monitor screens (plasma screens) placed at the back of the room, presidential prompters, or a combination of the two, depending on the size of the room. Again, you'll want the screens positioned to seem invisible, while letting you turn to at least three areas of the audience. The type and number of monitors you need will be determined by the size of the audience, the size of the room, and your ability to read from a distance.

Outdoor Presentation

When speaking to a live audience outdoors, you will probably use two or more presidential prompters. They can be positioned close to you without being obvious to the audience. That way, even if the audience size grows during your presentation, you'll be able to make eye contact with each section. Often an opaque backing is used to prevent sunlight or sky-light reflections toward the audience.

TIPS FROM THE PROS

> The burning question remains: "How will I know whether or not my teleprompting service provider will have a prompter bright enough for outdoors?" There is one fail-safe way to find out: ASK THEM FOR A DEMO! If they shy away from a demo or put you off, chances are pretty good they can't produce the goods.
> — STEVE GRAHAM, PC PROMPTING

Working outdoors can create a problem with the readability of the type. You can ask the teleprompter operator to change the screen from a black background with white letters to a white background with black letters, which often makes it easier to read the text in natural light. You may also want to change the background of the type if you are presenting on camera.

Once you have determined the appropriate type and number of monitors, communicate with the event coordinators to confirm that they have access to the equipment you need. You don't want any last minute surprises!

CHAPTER 3

The Teleprompter Operator

As I mentioned earlier, the teleprompter operator is vital to a successful teleprompted presentation. This section will help you to take full advantage of your prompter operator's skills.

Hiring a Teleprompter Operator

Typically, the event coordinators will provide you with a teleprompter operator. However, if you must handle this on your own, the best way to find an operator is to ask colleagues or local stage or film production people for recommendations. The International Alliance of Theatrical and Stage Employees (IATSE) local in your area should also be able to provide you with names. When you contact the recommended operator, you should ask the following questions:

- Have you prompted this type of project before?
- How long have you been teleprompting?
- How much set-up time do you need?
- What type of equipment do you use?
- Do you have back-up computers?
- Are you able to print out a corrected script?
- Do you have references?

Once you get satisfactory answers to these questions, you should still check the operator's references. It is essential to ask if the person is highly skilled, responsive to the presenter's needs, and able to work well under pressure. Remember, the better the operator, the smoother the presentation.

Coordinating with the Teleprompter Operator

The teleprompter operator's job is to help you look professional and confident. However, it is your job to help the operator help you.

Supply the operator with a complete copy of your script at least 24 hours before you begin working together. This will allow enough time for the loading of the script into the computer and into the teleprompter program. Ask the operator what file format is needed (generally a Word file) and on to what medium he or she needs it saved (floppy, CD, flash drive or even e-mail). You should also send a printed copy for the operator's reference.

Ask if the operator can arrange to have a back-up computer for the teleprompter in case of any problems. Though problems are rare, if a computer goes down, it's good to have a spare that can be immediately put into use.

CHAPTER 4
Before the Rehearsal

IT'S IMPORTANT THAT YOU ARE so familiar with your script that you can anticipate each word. That way, nothing that appears on the teleprompter will seem unfamiliar or catch you by surprise. To reach that level of familiarity requires a lot of prep time, so do not wait until you get to the presentation site. As soon as possible, start practicing with your paper script. Become familiar with it well before you see it on the teleprompter.

It is critical to understand that even if you have written every word of the script yourself, the words can seem unfamiliar when you are saying them aloud. Practice reading your script out loud over and over again. Read it to a test audience — family, friends, coworkers — to see if it makes sense to them. Have them give you honest feedback. Ask if your presentation is easy to follow and if it holds their attention. This will not only let you practice reading before an audience, it also may help you fine-tune your content.

Another way to practice is by reading in front of a mirror. Maintain eye contact with yourself in the mirror as much as possible. Look down only when you need the next phrase. Even though you won't be reading from the written page when you actually do your presentation, this exercise will help you determine how familiar you are with your script. The more you see your face in the mirror, the better able you'll be to engage an audience. You may want to tape your rehearsal and review it, focusing on eye contact and delivery.

Rehearsing on your own also gives you the opportunity to overcome the fear of making mistakes. From time to time during your practice, you will undoubtedly lose your place or stumble over your words. Welcome these errors. They train you to think on your feet. Use your knowledge of the topic to improvise or rephrase. Then work your way back to the script as smoothly as possible. It's far better to have these experiences during practice than to experience them for the first time in front of your audience. The more time you spend practicing independently, the smoother your rehearsal with the prompter will go and the better your performance will be.

In the chapter on do-it-yourself teleprompters, I have listed a number of affordable teleprompters that you could use to practice your presentation. Some give you the capability to record your presentation, which will let you evaluate your performance.

Script Copy

Even when using a teleprompter, it's critical to have a current copy of your script with you in case there's a problem. At the very least having the script will give you a feeling of security. You might chose to look at the script from time to time to give the impression that you have memorized the speech. Ask the teleprompter operator to include the page number on the prompter to keep you on track.

3 X 5 Cards

However, if you really know your subject, you can get away with using 3" x 5" note cards. The best way to prepare these cards is to find the keywords that represent each section of your presentation. Write each one on a separate card. Always number the cards in case they get out of order. The keywords will allow you to stay on track. Give the teleprompter operator a copy of the script with your keywords noted; that way, if the computer fails, the operator can find where you are in the presentation.

CHAPTER 5

At the Rehearsal

AN EXPERIENCED TELEPROMPTER OPERATOR will have read through your entire script making adjustments that will help make you more comfortable with your presentation. These may include:

- Inserting extra space between completed ideas
- Using bullet points in lists
- Changing formal language to spoken language (for example, "it is" becomes "it's")
- Inserting directions (such as "pause" or "turn to the slave monitor") that are clearly distinguished from your speech (placed in parentheses, italicized or indicated in color)
- Correcting spelling and typing errors
- Adding punctuation to make phrasing more natural

When you arrive for rehearsal, take the time to become acquainted with the teleprompter operator. Your aim is to create a good working relationship. An operator who knows that you respect and appreciate the value he or she brings to your performance will go the extra mile to cooperate with you and help make you look good. Remember, this is an expert who has dealt with a host of speakers and knows what works.

Once the operator is prepared and the prompter is loaded, you should sit together and read through the script. Sitting with the operator, rather than standing onstage or in front of the camera, will allow you to work together with the fewest distractions and interruptions. What's more, the other technical people (stagehands, sound and/or video crew) can continue doing their own jobs. As you read through the script, point out anything that is awkward for you to read. The following details are important to check:

- **Font size** (size of letters) — Is it too small or too large? Usually a medium font size is best (58-point Arial). The font size affects how many words are on a line. Too many words may cause side-to-side eye movement (scanning). Too few words won't allow you see what's coming next.

- **Color** — What works best? Most people find it easier to read white text against a black background, but you may prefer the reverse. If there is a dialogue with two or more people, the portion for each person can be displayed in a different color.

- **Numbers** — Do you prefer to have them written out as you say them? For instance, "1,564" may be written as "one thousand, five hundred, sixty-four" or as "fifteen hundred sixty-four." Also, numbers under 10 are usually spelled out, while 10 and over are frequently typed as numerals. Tell the operator what you prefer.

- **Symbols** — Are they confusing? You may prefer to have them written out like numbers, for example, "percent" instead of "%." This is especially useful if the symbol precedes the word, as in "$4,502." Instead, you might want to change it to read "4,502 dollars" or "four thousand, five hundred, two dollars," whichever way is easier for you.

- **Reminders**—Will you want to insert them? For example, ask to have "pause" or "turn to Camera 2" written out and set in a different font or color to cue you.
- **Capital letters for emphasis**—Would you like key words written in all CAPITAL LETTERS? Typically, scripts use both upper and lower case letters, so words in all caps will stand out and help you remember to emphasize them. However, be aware that capitalized words can be harder to read.
- **Script page numbers** — Would you like to have the script page numbers displayed on the prompter? This could prove helpful to stay on track when you're using a hard copy of your script at the podium.

The essential point is that you determine what markings will make the script easiest for you to read and review these corrections with the prompter operator. Additional changes may be needed later, but you can save a good deal of time and your rehearsal will go more smoothly if you make as many changes as possible before you begin.

TIPS FROM THE PROS

Ask your operator to adjust the font size until you can read it comfortably.
— RIP RADCLIFF, DIRECTOR

Hand Signals and Verbal Cues

Work out hand signals that you can use during your performance to let the operator know if you are having a problem.

Be prepared to signal:
- I've lost my place.
- Slow down.
- Speed up.
- Skip the next point.
- My monitor is not working.

Working out these hand signals will make you feel safe, even if you don't use them. Your hand signals should be visible to your operator, but they should not distract the audience.

You can also work out subtle verbal cues for the operator. During your presentation, you might say to the audience, "Let's slow down for a moment" to cue the operator to slow down. Or you could say, "I'm going to get off track for a moment and share a story with you," which will tell the operator to stop scrolling the script. "Let's move on" would then signal the operator that you're ready to return to the script.

Print Out Refined Script

After the operator has made all the changes to your script, ask for a paper copy. You want to have the latest copy available to you in case there is any problem with the monitor or the operator's computer. If you are at a podium, you can flip the pages as you move through your script in the same way newscasters do. This will ensure that you can seamlessly move on with your presentation without having to search for the right page.

ONCE YOU'VE READ THROUGH the script with the operator and made the necessary adjustments, it's time for the formal rehearsal. Ideally, you should rehearse in the place where you will deliver the presentation. This will more closely simulate what you will experience during your performance. This is especially important when you work with multiple monitors because you need to practice turning from monitor to monitor, reading the line indicated by the pointer. Your movements will then feel more natural, and you can determine whether the monitors are well placed and easy to read.

Rehearsing in your presentation position will be your first chance to read the script from the teleprompter without being able to turn to the operator. At this point you become solely in charge of the read. Rehearsing allows you to assess how well the teleprompter operator works with you. Experienced operators know that the presenter should control the pace of the read. They follow you; when you pause, they wait for you to start again. If you digress from the script, they wait for you to return to it. If you paraphrase, they move with you as if you were reading verbatim. The formal rehearsal is also the time to practice your hand signals or verbal cues. Remember, though your operator has more experience than you when it comes to prompting, it is your responsibility to clearly signal what you need. Rehearsing gives you the opportunity to build trust in your operator and confidence in yourself.

I cannot overstate the importance of practicing and rehearsing, both independently and with the teleprompter operator. It's a good deal of work, but it makes all the difference in the quality of your presentation. When you feel at ease and can approach your performance with the expectation of success, you can enjoy your presentation. That will have an enormous impact on your audience.

CHAPTER 7
Presentation Tips

THE FOLLOWING SUGGESTIONS will help ensure that your teleprompted presentation is more relaxed and effective. Some take a few minutes; others take only a few seconds. Use these techniques before you begin your presentation.

Visualization

Visualization, or guided imagery, is a technique that sports stars have used for decades. Tiger Woods' father taught him to create a mental image of the golf ball going into the hole. Michael Jordan, Jean-Claude Killy, and scores of other athletes play movies in their minds envisioning every detail of a perfect game and imagining how it feels to perform flawlessly. Visualization is also an excellent technique to prepare for your presentation with the teleprompter. Sit quietly and review your entire presentation in your mind. Picture yourself walking confidently to the podium or camera. See the audience responding enthusiastically. Imagine that everything works perfectly.

Relaxation

These are the techniques that seasoned performers use before they go onstage or on camera. You may feel uncomfortable the first few times you try these exercises, but believe me, they will make a huge difference in the way your audience perceives you. Feeling tension before and during your presentation is inevitable for almost everyone. But unconscious stress can reduce your effectiveness. Stress can cause you to hold your breath, slouch, speak too quickly and avoid eye contact. The following techniques will help minimize your stress:

Deep breathing

Most people are unaware that they are holding their breath, but this exercise will not only relax you but also allow you to take in much-needed oxygen, an essential element for clear thinking. Simply take a deep breath and release it slowly. Repeat twice. Then return your breathing to normal.

Isometric exercises

With your arms stretched forward, press your hands against a wall or on a table with all your strength. Hold for a few seconds; then release your muscles. This opens up your chest and shoulders and gives your voice more power.

Tense your face, squeezing every part to make your face as tight as possible. Tense your neck and bring your shoulders up toward your ears. Then slowly relax your muscles. The tightening and slow release of muscles will reduce tension.

Immediately before you begin, touch your fingertips together gently. Press hard for a few seconds; then let go. This will relax you, but your audience will not be aware of it. You can even do this when you are onstage before you begin to speak.

Vocal Warm-ups

The following exercises will give your voice greater power and allow you to speak more easily:

Yawning

Yawn widely a few times to relax your face and throat. Then, while yawning try speaking or counting to ten. Next, count or speak just thinking of a yawn without actually doing it. This will open your throat.

Humming

Warm up your voice with a hum. Hum gently. When you feel a slight vibration, start to play with different notes. Hum a tune. Think of this process as a massage of your vocal chords.

Diction exercises

Memorize or write these phrases on a slip of paper. Practice reading them aloud.

> Lah dah dee tee
> I like to look at lovely lanes and lawns
> Rubber baby buggy bumpers
> Red leather, yellow leather
> The lips, the teeth, the tip of the tongue

Water

Drink some room temperature water and have it nearby during your presentation. It will allow you your full voice.

Avoid Caffeine

Avoid drinking caffeinated beverages or eating chocolate before your presentation—these restrict the vocal chords.

Apple

If you have a dry mouth, eat a few bites of apple before you go onstage or on camera. Make sure you chew thoroughly.

Smile

A smile will open the throat and have a positive effect on your tone of voice.

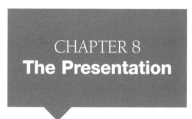

CHAPTER 8
The Presentation

ONCE YOU ARE FULLY PREPARED, it's time for you to relax and enjoy sharing your presentation with the audience. Remember, the teleprompter is there to make it easier for you.

Audio Support

If you'll be in a large auditorium or outdoors and the teleprompter operator will not be close enough to hear you, be sure there is audio support for the operator. Without sound, the operator can't follow you! It is most desirable to have the operator positioned within earshot. However, if circumstances prevent close positioning, make sure there is a clean sound feed via an audio monitor or headphones. Check this with the producer or teleprompter operator before the presentation.

Ad-libs

Once you become experienced at using the teleprompter, you will have more freedom during your presentation. Those who have worked with a prompter for years stray from the script, adding words, paraphrasing and ad-libbing. They feel free to include ideas or personal anecdotes. They can do this because they have rehearsed so thoroughly that they know how to return to the script seamlessly. They also know how to lead the operator back into the script by finishing their ad-lib with a verbatim reading of the text.

Natural Speech

The best speakers know that no one wants to listen to you just read, even though, in reality, you are reading. Your task is to become so natural at reading your script that you appear to be just talking. This "talking" becomes compelling when you show energy and enthusiasm for your subject. As with any good performance, your pace, inflection, and pitch should vary. A steady pace or a monotone puts an audience to sleep. In normal conversation, you speed up and slow down, you raise and lower your voice, and you pause to think of how you want to say things or to emphasize a point. The same should be true when you read from a teleprompter. The teleprompter should not be an obstacle between you and your audience; it should be the link that connects you.

Using Pauses

As I said earlier, pausing helps you sound more natural. Use pauses to build a sense of drama, to let your audience absorb your point, or to emphasize an important idea. A pause is also an excellent way to slow down if you sense that you are speaking too fast. Pausing allows you to catch your breath, regain focus, or find your place on the teleprompter should you get lost. A pause is a perfect time to make direct eye contact with your audience.

It's a good idea to practice using pauses to become comfortable using them. Pauses can last longer than you might think. We tend to overestimate their length, because silence often feels uncomfortable. When used effectively, a pause can last up to five seconds and still seem perfectly natural to your audience. Remember, you can tell your teleprompter operator to insert pause cues into your script.

Natural Enthusiasm

Often, when people use the teleprompter, they become so focused on reading the words correctly that they lose their natural enthusiasm. They forget their intent, the meaning of the presentation. This is a serious problem since it leads to a lifeless presentation which lacks the power to connect with the audience.

To maintain your energy, keep your mind on the purpose of your presentation. This purpose-focused approach is something I stress in my sales and presentation skills workshops. This is equally important to being effective while using a teleprompter. Remember that you are selling something — an idea, a process, a plan. Enthusiasm is contagious and an essential element of selling. To get a sense of the level of enthusiasm you need in your presentation, try this: Retell the story of an amazing experience you had to a friend, co-worker, or family member. Notice how you are feeling while you are doing this. That energy that you are feeling is your natural enthusiasm. Remind yourself to maintain that same level of energy when you make your presentation to your audience.

CHAPTER 9

Live Presentation Tips

Eye contact

When speaking to a live audience using either presidential prompters or a combination of presidential prompters and plasma screens, be sure to use all the prompters. This will allow you to make direct contact with all sections of your audience. Inexperienced speakers seem to jump from one prompter to another as if they were watching a tennis match. Your focus should move naturally between the prompters. There are different ways to accomplish this.

IPS FROM THE PROS

The key to natural prompter work is to read a sentence in your head and say the first half to the audience, and then read the second half while glancing up at the end.

— MICHAEL LEE, SPEAKER

The following recommendation is risky because it requires you to memorize or paraphrase a sentence or two for each shift between monitors. This technique is only effective for people who are comfortable with memorization. Start by looking at the prompter to your right. Complete a thought. Now, shift your attention to the space between the two prompters. Share a sentence or two that you have memorized or can paraphrase. Next, turn your head to the prompter on your left for your next complete thought. This method allows you to connect with three different sections of your audience. Never switch prompters in midthought. Doing so is very distracting to your audience. Completing each thought before you move actually adds to your effectiveness. Practice this technique until it feels natural.

If memorization is out of the question and you are not comfortable paraphrasing, consider the use of two presidential prompters with a large monitor centered at the back of the room. Again, move from one prompter to another after completing your thought. Use pauses to help you maintain a comfortable pace.

Movement

Balance your stance and maintain good posture. Make sure your physical presentation matches your message. For example, if your topic is serious, your body language shouldn't be casual. If your topic is humorous, you don't want to appear rigid.

TIPS FROM THE PROS

A top image wrecker is to have hands in pockets, constantly jiggling with loose change or keys. Remove all bits and pieces from pockets.

— LESLIE EVERETT, AUTHOR,
    PERSONAL BRANDING CONSULTANT

Don't move for the sake of moving. Pacing is distracting. Make your moves purposeful. Use movement to emphasis a point, to connect with a section of your audience, or to focus attention. Use your hands to gesture naturally. Let your gestures be an extension of your message. Don't put your hands in your pockets or cross your arms, because you will appear to be closing yourself off from your audience.

CHAPTER 10
On-Camera Tips

Eye contact

When using a camera mounted prompter, it's simple to make good eye contact with your audience. You simply read the script. Read the line that is noted by the pointer. It is usually slightly above dead center which allows those in the audience to feel that you are looking directly at them.

When using multiple cameras and/or multiple prompters, finish your thought before you turn your head or shift body position. Never sneak a look by shifting the eyes prior to the head movement. Such eye movement destroys the illusion of addressing the audience and signals that the speaker is uncomfortable.

When others are with you on camera, slave monitors can help you appear to be looking at them. The placement of a slave monitor or monitors is determined by the camera shots being used. The goal is to align your sightline with the monitor so that the shot makes you appear to be looking at the other person or people on the set though you are actually reading from the monitor. The slave monitor should be placed so that you can read it easily. You should finish your thought while looking at your camera and then turn to the slave monitor when addressing the other people on the set.

Prompter Placement

If your prompter cannot be mounted on the camera, you should experiment with its placement. The prompter needs to be positioned to allow those in the audience to feel that you are looking directly at them. When space allows, the prompter should be placed directly below and as close to the lens as possible. If it must be located to the side of the camera, it is best to place it as near as possible to the lens and at the same height as the lens. Do not move your eyes from the prompter to the camera lens. Your prompter eye line will be established as your point of focus. Even a slight shift in your gaze will be distracting and can make your audience feel uncomfortable. More importantly, it makes you look untrustworthy and will draw attention to the fact that you are reading.

Do not have a television monitor that is showing your live presentation within your line of vision. Even the most polished presenters will be tempted to glance at themselves in the monitor. The slightest glance will be visible and distracting to your audience. If you want to see how you look, simply ask to view a playback of your presentation.

On-Camera Clothing Tips

It is important to find out if your presentation is going to be recorded on tape or film. If taped, you must avoid wearing certain colors or patterns. Pure white tends to be so bright that it distracts the viewer. Black becomes so dense that all clothing details are lost. Red can appear to "bleed." Small patterns like houndstooth seem to vibrate.

Avoid large, shiny jewelry, because it can reflect the lights in the studio. Make sure that your jewelry doesn't clunk against the lapel microphone. Some silk ties and scarves can also create noise for the microphones.

Occasionally, you'll be placed in front of a special blue or green background (referred to simply as "blue-screen" or "green-screen"), which allows technical staff to electronically replace the background color with a different image. Because of the technology used, you must be aware of the color of the background that will be keyed out and avoid wearing that color. In other words, don't wear blue if you are appearing in front of a blue-screen or green if the background is green. Consider bringing alternate outfits to the set.

Types of Camera Shots

There are several different types of shots to use on camera. It is important for you to know how the camera operator plans to frame you, because your delivery should vary according to the type of camera shot.

Head Shot

A head shot frames you from a couple of inches above your head down to the knot of your tie for a man or approximately the same spot for a woman. This shot works effectively when you're appearing on television or any type of small screen, but if your image is projected onto a large screen it is a terrible shot. Your head will seem gigantic, as if you were the Great Oz.

When framed in a head shot, you absolutely should not use your hands. They won't be visible, and all the audience will see is your shoulders moving, which makes you appear nervous. However, if the headshot is mixed with longer shots, it's fine to use your hands because your movements will be seen and understood in context.

Head shots require your delivery to be intimate. Speak as if you were having a one-on-one conversation.

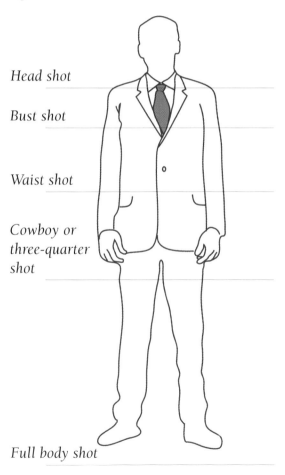

Head shot

Bust shot

Waist shot

Cowboy or three-quarter shot

Full body shot

Bust Shot

A bust shot frames you from a few inches above your head down to midchest. This shot is good for interviews or for delivering particularly important messages. Just as with the head shot, your hands will not be visible, so keep them still. With a bust shot, your delivery will not be quite as intimate as with a head shot. Talk to the camera as if you were talking to people across a small table.

Waist Shot

A waist shot frames you from a few inches above your head down to your waist. This is also good framing for interviews. Most presenters prefer this shot since it allows them to use their hands naturally. However, you should not shift your body below the waist unless the camera is following you as you walk. This framing allows you to speak with greater energy and power than the shots described above.

TIPS FROM THE PROS

If you tend to be jittery when standing, you can ask to sit on the edge of a desk or stool.

— RIP RADCLIFF, DIRECTOR

Cowboy or Three-quarter Shot

A cowboy or three-quarter shot frames you from a few inches above your head down to midthigh (where your holster would be if you were a cowboy—hence the name). This framing allows you to move more freely than in the previously described shots. Address the camera as if you were speaking to a roomful of people.

Full body

As you've probably assumed, a full body shot frames you from a few inches above your head down to your toes. This framing allows movement of the whole body. As the shot encompasses more of your body, your gestures must become larger and your vocal energy fuller, though not necessarily louder.

Physical Presentation

Balance your stance and maintain good posture. Make sure your physical presentation matches your message. Hold your position; if you move, it will make the camera operator move to follow you. If you shift your weight, you'll distract the audience from your message.

If you are concerned about your weight or size, present your body at a slight angle but keep your face full front.

If you wear glasses, consider purchasing contacts or non-reflective lenses to assure a glare-free shot. If necessary, the camera operator can tilt your glasses slightly to reduce glare. If you have a spare set of glasses or contacts, bring them, in case something should happen to your regular ones.

TIPS FROM THE PROS

In order for the shot to be lit before you get there, let your director know what color your hair is, if you wear glasses, are bald, or have any physical issues regarding movement or standing.

— TODD MITZMAN, DIRECTOR

CHAPTER 11

What to Do When Things go Wrong

EVEN AFTER YOU HAVE done everything you need todo to have a successful presentation, things can still go wrong. However, if you have rehearsed enough to be truly comfortable with your script, you should be fine. This section provides guidance about what to do when things go wrong. But don't worry — problems rarely occur.

The Teleprompter's Computer Freezes

As you no doubt already know, when you use technology, things can go wrong. If a problem arises, trust that your teleprompter operator is doing everything to solve the problem. Often this involves rebooting the computer or going to a back-up computer. To prepare for the possibility of a breakdown, always make sure that you have your script or cue cards on hand for reference. Do not panic. Remember that you have a message to convey to your audience and stay focused. If you are unable to have a script at hand, you should ad-lib until the computer comes back up. It is reasonable to expect a three-to-five-minute delay for the computer to reboot. That's a lot of time to fill. This situation is a good example of why it's so important to really know your subject.

You Ad-lib and Lose Your Train of Thought

When you ad-lib or go "off script," you can lose your place on the teleprompter. You'll need to think on your feet. Improvise—you might rephrase the last idea you remember saying before you started ad-libbing. Even if it turns out that wasn't the very last point, it will give the teleprompter operator a clue about where to cue up. If you see that you have already said the words on the monitor, paraphrase the ideas and continue paraphrasing until you get back to where you originally left off. Then you will be able to return to reading.

Your Text is Scrolling Too Fast or Too Slow

If your script is being scrolled at a pace that's uncomfortable for you, let the operator know. This is where a predetermined hand signal or subtle verbal cue will be helpful. If you haven't discussed a signal, take a breath and try to regain control of the pace. You can best accomplish this by pausing, which will give the operator time to catch up with you or force him or her to slow down.

The Monitor Stops Working

On rare occasions a monitor will go blank. Usually the problem is as simple as a cord that has become loose or a button that has been accidentally bumped. A crew member can fix this easily, but first you need to alert your teleprompter operator with a hand signal you worked out previously. Remember, your signal should be clear to the operator but not obvious to your audience. When your signal is acknowledged, take a deep breath and continue your presentation using ad-libs or referring to your script until the problem is solved.

Words are Being Cut Off on the Screen

Sometimes the monitor cuts off the ends of words on the right side of the screen. Generally, you fix this problem during rehearsal, but if it arises during your presentation, simply complete the words as best you can. You can usually determine the letter or letters that are missing based on the context in which the word is being used. When in doubt, paraphrase.

If All Else Fails

If a problem arises and the operator doesn't respond or understand your hand signals, you may need to simply explain the situation to the audience. Let them know you are in control by saying something like, "I'm having a technical problem here. My teleprompter isn't working. I'll just talk to you while they get the system working again." If you're comfortable with humor, you can make light of the situation, which will put the audience at ease.

CHAPTER 12

Innovative Methods of Teleprompting

Hub Schlafly, inventor of the teleprompter, says "that Barton's original idea for the teleprompter, a name he coined, was for use as a 'prompter'. Today, while some still use it for that purpose, most users — newscasters, commentors, politicians and others use it as a 'reader.' Some however use it simply as an index and sequence reminder for their talking points."

Clocks

In 1952, Bishop Fulton Sheehan used the teleprompter to display a clock. He was a great extemporaneous speaker, but he wanted to make sure he stayed on track and finished on time. If you can speak well without a script, this is a great idea.

Bullet Points

Other speakers use bullet points on the teleprompter. They know their material well, but have a problem sounding natural when they read a script or simply don't want to be tied to one. If either of these situations applies to you, consider this method.

PowerPoint

One of the problems with PowerPoint presentations is that both the speaker and the audience are focused on the screen. To be effective, you need the audience to stay connected to you. Display your PowerPoint presentation on the teleprompter. That way the audience can look at the screen and you can maintain eye contact with your audience. Steer your audience's attention to the screen by glancing at it; then draw their focus back to you by returning your eye contact to them.

Pictograms

For some highly visual people, pictograms are an effective way of staying on track during a presentation. A pictogram is an image (photo, drawing, etc.) that represents a key idea in your presentation. Use pictograms on your teleprompter as you would bullet points. Just replace the ideas in the bullet points with images that represent them.

CHAPTER 13
Do-It-Yourself
Teleprompting

THERE ARE TOOLS that are helpful for people who want to learn how to use the teleprompter effectively, but can't afford to hire an entire crew. They're especially useful for vloggers (video online weblog presenters), who tend to have such problems as rambling or losing eye contact with their audience. The following tools are simple, effective, and affordable. They allow you the freedom to rehearse and create in your free time.

Serious Magic™

Serious Magic has created great software for people who want an inexpensive but effective method for making their own video presentation. It can also be used as a rehearsal tool. Serious Magic offers a number of teleprompter application products that are simple to use. You can type your script into the on-screen

TIPS FROM THE PROS

Practice positioning the camcorder and the computer at a distance. Then use the camcorder to zoom in. After finding the appropriate distance and with some practice, it will appear that you're looking directly into the camera; when, in fact, you're looking at the computer screen. This is what I use with Serious Magic and it works very well.

— TERRY BROCK, SPEAKER

teleprompter or just cut and paste from another program, such as Microsoft Word. The automated teleprompter scrolls your script, and you read the words as they pass through a red translucent bar. You can adjust the speed of the scroll. You can also pause to speak extemporaneously without losing your place. If you want to view your presentation, connect a camera to your computer and record it.

Telestreamer™

The folks at Prompter People have produced a great new tool for a do-it-yourself prompter that combines an integrated teleprompter and camera that can be connected to your computer. Called the Telestreamer, this device works perfectly with Serious Magic's products, allowing in-the-lens eye contact.

Homemade prompters

Plasti-Prompter2

This is probably the most inexpensive teleprompter ever invented. Created by Max Rottersman, this system calls for nothing more than two open CD cases, binder clips, and some inexpensive software. And it really works! Check out his plan at www.wallstreetfree thinker.com.

TIPS FROM THE PROS

Be aware that when using an inexpensive home-made teleprompter, the type on the prompter screen may jitter. The pupil of the eye will instinctively react to the movement and your eyes will also appear jittery.

— JOANNE CARMADA, LISTEC VIDEO

CHAPTER 14
Global Teleprompting Use

IF YOU ARE TAKING a teleprompter to a country other than your own, you need to know the type of video system, power supply, and plug that is standard in that country. Some countries' video standards include NTSC, PAL, and Secam.

You also need to be sure that your teleprompter operator has the appropriate software to scroll in your language. You may need a conversion system for the text, depending on what program was used for creating your script.

If your teleprompter operator is not fluent in the language you are reading, make sure that you stick to the script verbatim. This allows a seasoned teleprompter operator to follow you.

CHAPTER 15
Dos & Don'ts

- **Do not:** Race the teleprompter — you will lose!
- **Do not:** Stare — you will look dazed or crazy.
- **Do not:** Move your head from side to side as you read.
- **Do not:** Let a mistake paralyze you — remember, you know your topic and your script.
- **Do not:** Forget to PRACTICE!!!!!!!!!!!!!!!!

- **Do:** Practice! Practice!! Practice!!!
- **Do:** Lead the pace of the teleprompter — you are in charge!
- **Do:** Vary your pace and pitch.
- **Do:** Add interjections when it feels natural to do so ("well", "oh", "as you can see", etc.)
- **Do:** Speak naturally — do not just read.
- **Do:** Pause for emphasis and drama.
- **Do:** Put energy behind your words.
- **Do:** See the prompter as a person — remember you are speaking to an audience.
- **Do:** Have fun!

CHAPTER 16
Success Checklist

❑ Did I send the script to the teleprompter operator at least 24 hours before the job?

❑ Did I spend time practicing the script out loud?

❑ Did I bring along any updates to the script?

❑ Did I sit with the teleprompter operator and make sure that the changes have been made to the script?

❑ Did the operator change symbols into words such as % to percent and $ to dollar?

❑ Did the operator change written language to verbal language such as "it is" to "it's"?

❑ Did the operator use a medium-sized font such as 58-point Arial?

❑ Did the operator print out a current copy of the script?

❑ Did I check to see if I can easily read all the words on the monitor?

❑ Did the operator and I establish hand signals or verbal cues for potential problems? (Faster, slower, monitor off, etc.)

❑ Did I go through a formal rehearsal with the operator?

Resource Guide

Achievement Systems Incorporated
Terry Brock,MBA, CSP
7550 Hinson Suite 15-c
Orlando, Florida 32819
terry@terrybrock.com
www.terrybrock.com
1.407.363.0505

Computer Prompting Systems
Joe O'Donell
Joe41865@wowway.com
1.586.939-6300

Ethno-Connect™
Michael Lee,MBA, CSP
P.O. Box 2488
Dublin, CA 94568
925.829.9700
925.905.0437
www.ethnoconnect.com
seminars@netvista.net

Lesley Everett
Personal Branding Consultant
Lesley@walkingtall.org
www.walkingtall.org
www.lesleyeverett.com
Telephone: +44 (0)1344 427977
Fax: +44 (0)1344 428071
Mobile: +44 (0)7778 551257

The Idea Nexus
Todd Mitzman
Director/Producer
www.ideanexus.net
248.345.7431

Listec Video
2001 Palm Beach Lakes Blvd, Suite 411
West Palm Beach, Florida 33409
561.683.3002
www.listec.com

PC Prompting
Steve Graham
prompter@aol.com
www.pcprompting.com
818.831.6554

Post 21
Cindy Schmidt
Teleprompter Operator and Closed Captioning
www.post21.tv
cindy@post21.tv
248.506.6907

Prompter People
22189 Old Santa Cruz Hwy
Los Gatos, California 95033
rene@prompterpeople.com
www.prompterpeople.com

Max Rottesman
www.wallstreetfreethinker.com
editor@wallstreetfreethinker.com

Serious Magic
101 Parkshore Dr Suite 250
Folsom, California 95630
916.985.8000
www.seriousmagic.com

Dawn Waldrup
dwaldrop@best-impressions.com
www.best-impressions.com
330.483.0411

About the Author

Laurie Brown started her career as an actor, working primarily in commercials and industrial films. She served on the national and executive boards of the Screen Actors Guild for 10 years.

Over nineteen years ago, Laurie began her career as a trainer, coach, and consultant. She has earned a reputation as a highly engaging and effective professional whose efforts get results for her clients. Her work has taken her across the United States and abroad working with culturally diverse audiences at all corporate levels. Laurie leads workshops on presentation and sales skills and coaches individuals to be more effective speakers.

Laurie's clients include: GM, Ford, GMAC, Visteon, Calumet Lubricants, BMW, Volkswagen, Kmart, UAW/GM, UAW/Delphi and UAW/Ford among others. Her excellent communication skills and supportive approach with learners have earned her the highest evaluations from trainees and clients alike.

Laurie is a member of the National Speakers Association, the American Society for Training and Development, American Federation of Television and Radio Artists and the Screen Actors Guild.

Contact Information

To contact Laurie about speaking engagements or consulting please
call:

877.999.DIFF
248.761.7510
248.545.7528 (fax)

Or e-mail: lauriebrown@thedifference.net

"The Teleprompter Manual"
Order Form

To order individual copies of the book:

    Call: The Difference Press/Consumer Sales at **877. 999.3433**

    or Order Online at **www.thedifference.net**

    or Fax this Form to: **248. 545.7528**

(1-5) COPIES @ $19.95 each

Postage and Handling: US/Canada $4.00 for one book, plus $2.00 for each additional book. International: $9.00 for one book, $5.00 for each additional book. (Estimate.) No cash/COD.

Number of Copies @ $19.95 _____   Total _____

Michigan Sales Tax: Add 6% (Michigan residents only) _____

                                    Postage and Handling _____

                                    Total Amount Due _____

Name _____

Address _____

City _____ State _____ Zip _____

Phone _____

Email _____

Charge My ____ Amex   ____ Visa   ____ Mastercard

Credit Card No. _____ Exp _____

Signature _____

Check or Money Order Payable to: The Difference

Mail to: The Difference
            P.O. Box 69046
            Pleasant Ridge, Michigan 48069

Please allow 3-4 weeks for US delivery; 4-6 weeks outside of the US.